WHAT GOD HAS FOR ME IS MINE

My Name Is on It

By Dr. Tonia Ann Walker

DEDICATION PAGE

This book is for every daughter of God who has walked through seasons of breaking, birthing, and becoming. To every student I have taught, every woman I have prayed for, and every soul God has assigned to my voice, for those who believed in me before I believed in myself.

Dr. Tonia Ann Walker: "I am coaching, motivating, and educating others through my lived experiences."

COPYRIGHT PAGE

ISBN: **979-8-9948042-0-9**

TABLE OF CONTENTS

INTRODUCTION

There was a time when the echo of my footsteps down the halls of the projects felt like the only rhythm my life would ever know. But God had other plans. He took me from those humble beginnings and led me into the halls of many Universities, places I never imagined I would belong. That journey was not easy or quick. But it was divine.

This book is my declaration of faith. It is a reminder that no matter where you start, no matter what odds are stacked against you, what God has ordained for your life is already yours. You do not have to beg for it. You do not have to compete for it. You must believe it and walk in it.

I wrote this for the ones who feel overlooked. For those who have been told they are too late, too broken, or too far behind. I want you to know you are not. You are exactly where you need to be for God to show you what he has had for you all along.

I wrote this for the dreamers who feel forgotten. For the faithful who are growing weary. For the ones who have watched doors close and wonder if they missed their moment. I want you to know you did not. You are right on time. And this journey you are on is not a mistake; it is preparation.

This book is not just a collection of words; it is a declaration. A spiritual reminder that no matter how long it takes, no matter how many detours you face, what God has ordained for your life cannot be stolen, delayed, or denied. It is already written. It is already yours.

Each chapter will walk you through the valleys and victories of claiming your divine portion. You will find stories, scriptures, and reflections that remind you of who you are and whose you are. You will be challenged to let go of comparison, embrace your identity, and walk boldly in the authority God has given you.

So, take a deep breath. Open your heart. And get ready to reclaim what is already yours.

"For I know the plans I have for you," declares the Lord, "plans to prosper you and not to harm you, plans to give you hope and a future." — Jeremiah 29:11

CHAPTER ONE:
FROM THE PROJECTS TO PURPOSE

I did not grow up with stained glass windows or Sunday brunches. I grew up with cracked concrete, sirens echoing through the night, and a front-row seat to survival. The housing projects were not just places; they were proving grounds. And while the world saw limitation, God saw preparation.

There was a hallway in my childhood building that smelled like fried urine and floor cleaner. I used to sit on the steps and dream of something bigger, something brighter. I did not know what it was, but I knew it had to exist. I did not realize then that what I was feeling was not just ambition, it was divine agitation. God was stirring something in me.

Years later, I walked into a university hallway for the first time. The floors were polished; the air smelled like books and possibility. I paused, overwhelmed, not by fear, but by gratitude. I was not supposed to be here. But I was. And not by luck, but by purpose.

"But those who hope in the LORD will renew their strength. They will soar on wings like eagles; they will run and not grow weary; they will walk and not be faint."— Isaiah 40:31

That scripture carried me through moments when I felt like an imposter, and I questioned whether I belonged. But God does not call the qualified; He qualifies the called. And I was called.

Faith Lesson

God does not need perfect conditions to begin a plan for your life. He starts where you are. He uses what you have. And He walks with you through every hallway, whether lined with broken tiles or ivy-covered bricks. Your beginning is not your boundary; it is your blueprint.

This truth became real for me as a young girl, dreaming about college in a world where few from my community even considered it. College felt so far away. I worried about funds, feared rejection, and doubted myself. But I kept my dream alive in my heart, and God was preparing a path I could not yet see.

At first, I attended Housatonic Community College nearby, but balancing work and family made it impossible to continue. Then I discovered non-traditional programs. A college in New York and Sacred Heart University in Connecticut offered a weekend university and an alternative schedule program. Sacred Heart University became the place where my journey truly began.

I would go on to earn my bachelor's degree in accounting, MBA, and DBA, whether through employment or education, I walked the halls of universities from Connecticut to Tennessee, including HBCU and Ivy League institutions. God not only opened the doors but orchestrated experiences that allowed me to embrace the full campus life, sometimes as a student, sometimes as an employee. Every hallway, every classroom, every challenge was part of His preparation.

Reflection Prompt

Think back to where your journey began.

- What places shaped your resilience?
- What moments whispered to you that there was more?

Write them down. Honor them. They are part of your testimony.

Closing Prayer

Lord, thank You for seeing me beyond my surroundings. Thank You for calling me even when I could not hear You clearly. Help me walk boldly in the purpose You have prepared, knowing that what You have for me is already mine. Amen.

CHAPTER TWO:
THE SHIFT WITHIN

I used to think change was something that happened around your new job, new zip code, new people. But real change? It starts inside. Before God moved me into new rooms, He moved me into a new mindset.

There was a season when everything looked the same on the outside. Same neighborhood. Same struggles. But something had shifted in me. I stopped asking *"Why me?"* and started asking *"What now, God?"* That shift was subtle, but it was sacred. It was the beginning of me seeing myself the way God saw me, not as a product of my past, but as a vessel for His promise.

"Do not conform to the pattern of this world but be transformed by the renewing of your mind." – Romans 12:2

Renewal is not a one-time event. It is a daily decision. I had to unlearn the lies I had been told that I was not enough, that I did not belong, that my background disqualified me. And I had to replace them with truth. God's truth.

Faith Lesson

I recall how blessed I was to land a job at General Electric (GE) in my early twenties, while still living in a housing project. It felt like a miracle. A woman from my church noticed my potential and told me GE was hiring. I remember hesitating, *could someone from my neighborhood really fit in there,* but I applied anyway. To my amazement, I was called for an interview...and then offered the job.

My time at GE was transformative. I was an accounting clerk handling accounts receivable for GE Supply, one of its many subsidiaries. Every day I walked into that office, I carried both excitement and nervousness. I was stepping into a world that felt so far removed from the cracked concrete of my childhood.

Around that same time, I had been praying for a new car. I had little hope, but I trusted God. One day, a co-worker from another state casually mentioned that GE had cars available for sale. Back then, there was no internet, only fax machines. And so, I received a faxed inventory list. My heart raced as I scanned cars I had never seen in person, prices I could barely imagine.

I remember pausing on one car: a champagne-colored, light pink Ford Taurus with about 39,000 miles. Could I really do this? It was a leap of faith buying a car sight unseen. But something inside me whispered, *"This is from God. Step forward."* I made the call. GE approved the loan. They even offered to have a driver deliver the car to my home, but I requested it be delivered from Houston, Texas, to GE in Bridgeport, Connecticut. Not my housing project.

That moment, so ordinary on paper, was extraordinary in my life. It was more than a car. It was a confirmation that God hears our prayers, even when the path seems impossible. That car carried me through many years of growth, faith, and new beginnings.

Around the same time, I began attending Sacred Heart University's Weekend Program. Balancing work, school, and life felt impossible at times, but God provided clarity and stamina. In my twenties, while working at GE, I purchased my first home, a condominium, proof that divine favor does not wait for perfect timing.

Through it all, I had to walk forward unapologetically. The projects were still real to me, but they no longer defined me. I held my head high in spaces where I once felt I didn't belong, trusting God's plan, and walking boldly in His purpose.

Reflection Prompt

What lies have you believed about yourself? Write them down. Then, beside each one, write a truth from scripture that replaces it. Speak those truths over yourself daily. That is how you renew your mind.

____

____

____

____

____

Closing Prayer

Lord, thank You for renewing my mind and restoring my identity. Help me to see myself the way You see me, and to walk boldly in the truth of who I am. Amen.

CHAPTER THREE:
BATTLES BEFORE BLESSINGS

I used to think that once I said "yes" to God's plan, everything would fall into place. But I quickly learned that obedience does not cancel opposition; it attracts it. The moment I started walking in purpose, the battles intensified. Doubt crept in. Distractions multiplied. Doors slammed shut. And I wondered, *if this is God's will, why is it so hard?*

Here is the truth: resistance is often confirmation. The enemy does not fight what is not a threat. And when you begin to claim what God has for you, you become a threat to every lie, every stronghold, and every generational curse that tried to keep you bound.

"No weapon formed against you shall prosper." — Isaiah 54:17

Notice it does not say weapons will not form. It says they will not prosper. That means you might feel the sting, but you will not be stopped. You might cry, but you will not quit. What God has for you is still yours, even in the middle of the battle.

Faith Lesson

Opposition is not a sign to turn back. It is a signal to press in. Every battle you face on the way to your blessing is building spiritual muscle. You are not just walking into purpose; you are being fortified for it.

I knew there was a stigma surrounding Father Panik Village (F.P.V.) in Bridgeport, CT. Just the thought of applying required faith. But I remembered this scripture:

"I planted, Apollos watered, but God gave the increase." — 1 Corinthians 3:6 (NKJV)

It reminded me that while human effort is important, God is the one who brings growth and transformation. A sister at my church encouraged me to apply to GE. I planted the seed, and God added the increase.

When I started at GE, my boss, a woman from Philadelphia, shared a story about my hiring. She had been trying to fill three positions and repeatedly checked with HR, but no applicants met the requirements. Finally, she asked to review applications herself. She pulled the three most recent applications, and two were from Bridgeport, CT.

I suspect she may not have realized the stigma surrounding Bridgeport or F.P.V., but she gave me a chance. I was hired. The other two hires, one from Bridgeport and another from Shelton, CT, had an English-language barrier. Though it was not my battle to fight, I stepped through a door that many assumed would remain closed.

Later, my boss shared her perspective about working in the City of Bridgeport but living in another city. In the City of Philadelphia, if someone worked there and did not live there, a city tax might apply. She said, *"I don't know what you're doing in Bridgeport, but this wouldn't happen in Philly."* God was blessing me through hidden favor and divine orchestration.

The weapon may be formed, but it will not prosper. God adds the increase, and His favor overrides every obstacle. Amen.

What God Has for Me, Is Mine: It Has My Name on It!

Reflection Prompt

What battles have you faced since stepping into your calling? Write them down. Then, beside each one, write how God showed up, or how you are trusting Him to show up. Your struggle is not wasted; it is part of your story.

____

____

____

____

____

Closing Prayer

Lord, thank You for being my defender in every battle. Help me stand firm, knowing that no weapon formed against me will prosper. Strengthen me for the fight and remind me that the blessing is still mine. Amen.

CHAPTER FOUR:

THE POWER OF IDENTITY

Before you can walk boldly in purpose, you must know who you are and whose you are. The enemy's greatest tactic is not destruction; it is confusion. If he can get you to question your identity, he can get you to forfeit your destiny.

I spent years trying to be what others expected. I wore masks. I chased applause. I shrank myself to fit into rooms I was never meant to enter. But purpose does not require performance; it demands alignment. And alignment begins with identity.

"You are a chosen people, a royal priesthood, a holy nation, God's special possession." — 1 Peter 2:9

You were not created to blend in. You were called to stand out. You carry divine DNA. When you walk into that truth, you stop seeking validation from broken places. You start showing up with authority, not apology.

Faith Lesson

Your identity is your weapon. When you know who you are, you stop negotiating with fear. You stop settling for less. You stop entertaining lies. You realize, *I am not just surviving; I am sent.*

God gives favor and authority to those aligned with Him:

"I have placed before you an open door, which no one can shut." — Revelation 3:8.

"I will place on his shoulder the key to the house of David; what he opens no one can shut, and what he shuts no one can open." — Isaiah 22:22:

"And so, find favor and high esteem in the sight of God and man." — Proverbs 3:4:

Alignment with God is less about perfection and more about direction, orienting your heart, mind, and actions toward divine truth.

Ways to Confirm Alignment with God:

Living According to God's Will

- Submit to divine wisdom rather than relying solely on your understanding.
- Seek God's guidance through prayer, scripture, and reflection.
- Obey His Word out of love and trust, not obligation.

Heart and Soul Alignment

- Let your spirit lead your soul and body, not emotions or worldly desires.
- Renew your mind with God's truth, letting your thoughts reflect His perspective.
- Find joy in God, not just in His blessings, but in His presence.

Realignment Through Challenges

- Life's difficulties can push you to realign with God.
- Affliction can serve as a spiritual "chiropractic adjustment," restoring your posture, upright, strong, and purposeful.

The Outcome

- Peace, clarity, and a deep sense of purpose.
- A life that flows smoothly, like coordinated gears.
- A transformative connection with God that changes how you live, love, and lead.

Daily Rhythms of Alignment:

- **Starting the Day with Prayer or Scripture:** Pause before the world, seek God's guidance first.

- **Speaking with Grace and Truth:** Speak truth in love, choose kindness over sarcasm.

- **Making Decisions with God in Mind**: Prioritize integrity over convenience, seek discernment.

- **Serving Others Without Expecting Recognition:** Give quietly, reflecting humility and compassion.

- **Responding to Stress with Faith:** Pause, pray, and trust God's timing.

- **Consuming Media with Discernment:** Guard your heart and mind; choose what draws you closer to God.

- **Handling Money with Stewardship:** Save and give wisely, seeing resources as gifts to bless others.

These are not rules; they are rhythms. When your daily life reflects God's heart, you walk in alignment. It is not about perfection; it is about intentionality.

Reflection Prompt

Where have you been shrinking to fit in? What lies have you believed about your worth? Write a declaration of truth over your life. Start with:

"I am..."

...and let God finish the sentence.

____

____

____

____

____

Closing Prayer

Father, thank You for calling me chosen. Help me to walk in the fullness of who You created me to be. Silence every lie and remind me daily that I am Yours. Amen.

CHAPTER FIVE:

THE TRAP OF COMPARISON

I remember scrolling through social media and seeing someone announce a promotion, another post about a new house, and yet another celebrating a milestone I had not reached. I didn't feel jealous, I felt behind. I started questioning my pace, my progress, even my purpose. But God gently reminded me: *"What I have for you is yours. You are not late. You are aligned."*

Comparison does more than distract; it distorts. It makes you forget the miracles in your own life because you are too busy counting someone else's. It turns purpose into performance and calling into competition. But God does not do duplicates. Your journey is custom-built for your growth, your gifts, and your impact.

"Let us run with perseverance the race marked out for us." — Hebrews 12:1

Your race is yours. Not theirs. And when you fix your eyes on Jesus, you stop measuring your worth by someone else's timeline.

"The race is not to the swift,
Nor the battle to the strong,
Nor bread to the wise,
Nor riches to men of understanding,
Nor favor to men of skill;
But time and chance happen to them all." — Ecclesiastes 9:11-18 (NKJV)

Faith Lesson

God's blessings are not scarce; they are specific. What he has for you is tailored to your assignment. When you embrace your lane, you stop swerving into someone else's.

Timing is everything, and God's timing is perfect. He prepares you for every blessing. I remember a moment while traveling internationally to a tropical island, in October 2016, I received a call that I had passed my oral defense and completed my doctorate. I wanted a gift, a blessing, a celebration that reflected this milestone. During this time, I mostly worked part-time and consulted while finishing my doctoral studies.

In my rare spare moments, I would stalk the Mercedes dealership at night, dreaming. I admired the sporty two-door models, sometimes even looking at BMWs in the adjoining lot, but my heart kept returning to the Mercedes. I wasn't just dreaming about a car; I was dreaming about God's favor, a generational blessing rooted in faithfulness, obedience, and the promises of God flowing through my bloodline.

One night, God gave me a dream about this specific Mercedes. This Mercedes was not on the lot, as I had frequented the dealership several nights a week. I looked everywhere for the Mercedes I saw in my dream. Then, one day, I saw it: a car exactly like the one from my dream, a sporty model with a square front and rounded back at the dealership. It was a 2014 Mercedes-Benz CLA250. It was a new model for Mercedes. I bought it at 27,000 miles, paying $30,000 on credit as my Doctoral Degree gift to myself for my major milestone. That car has been a long-lasting blessing, fully paid off, and still a testament to God's faithfulness. Friends, strangers, and even the dealership asked to buy it still, while acknowledging the favor in my life. Some strangers even say I have next, and it still gets a lot of compliments. I have had other cars, never one as long-lasting as this one. What God has for me is mine. It has my name on it, and it cannot be duplicated.

Reflection Prompt

Where have you been comparing your journey to someone else's? Write down three things God has done for you that you may have overlooked. Celebrate them. They are evidence of His hand on your life.

Closing Prayer

Lord, thank You for the unique path You have carved for me. To stay focused on my assignment and trust the timing. Free me from comparison and fill me with contentment. Amen.

CHAPTER SIX:
WHEN GOD CLOSES A DOOR

There is a moment in every journey when something ends, a job, a relationship, a dream you thought was yours. And it hurts. You wonder if you missed it, messed it up, or misunderstood the assignment. But sometimes, a closed door is not rejection; it is redirection.

I remember praying for something I thought was perfect. I fasted, believed, and waited. And then... silence. No breakthrough. Just a door that would not budge. I felt abandoned. But later, I saw what I could not see then: that closed door protected me from something I was not ready for. God was not punishing me; He was positioning me.

"See, I have placed before you an open door that no one can shut." — Revelation 3:8

God does not slam doors and leave you stranded. He closes them to guide you to the one that opens into purpose, peace, and provision.

Faith Lesson

Closed doors are not the end of your story. They are divine edits. Trust the Author. He knows the plot twist that is coming next.

It took me a long time to learn this. I used to mourn every closed door, even when it wasn't good for me. But now I understand: each closed door brings a lesson, a blessing, and preparation for the next opportunity.

When I was around nineteen, my first job was at Mechanics and Farmers Bank as a TEFRA Clerk, sending backup withholding to the IRS. From there, I went to General Electric (GE). Many blessings came through GE, but after four years, that door closed. There was an opportunity to move to the South with the company, but I wasn't ready. I had small children and no support system. So, I stayed.

I had my car from GE, started the Weekend University program at SHU, and even purchased a condominium right out of the projects, all in my twenties. GE offered a severance package, and I asked if I could receive an early payment to continue my studies. I used my tuition reimbursement as a down payment on my condominium. Human Resources stepped in and again paid my tuition to SHU, exceeding my expectations and allowing me to continue with my schooling, while the door was closing. God's favor was evident: *"Favor isn't fair."* I was honest with HR about what I did with the original tuition reimbursement.

After GE, I began working for Automatic Data Processing (ADP), a company I fondly call a "cash cow," a source of consistent blessings. ADP provided tuition reimbursement, employee stock options, travel opportunities, training, car purchases, and more. During this season, I bought two cars, invested in stock that split three times, and built a house.

Eventually, ADP consolidated, and that door closed, too. But by this time, I had accepted closed doors. I no longer questioned them; I trusted the Lord.

"Trust in the LORD with all your heart and lean not on your own understanding; in all your ways acknowledge Him, and He will direct your paths." — Proverbs 3:5-6

What Closed Doors Can Represent Spiritually:

- **Protection:** Sometimes a door is closed to shield us from what isn't meant for us. What appears to be denial may be divine safeguarding.
- **Redirection:** A closed door can guide us toward a better path. It is not the end; it is a pivotal point.
- **Growth Opportunity:** Waiting at a closed door builds patience, trust, and perseverance. It strengthens your faith muscles.

"What He opens no one can shut, and what He shuts no one can open." — Revelation 3:7

Closed doors are not failure; they are divine guidance.

Reflection Prompt

Think of a closed door in your life. What did it teach you? What did it protect you from? Then write a letter to that moment, thanking it for what it revealed.

____

____

____

____

____

Closing Prayer

Lord, thank You for every door You have closed. Help me to trust Your wisdom even when I do not understand. Give me peace in transition and faith for what is ahead. Amen.

CHAPTER SEVEN:
THE WILDERNESS OF WAITING

Waiting is hard. It is the space between the promise and the fulfillment, where prayers feel unanswered, and progress seems invisible. But waiting is not wasted; it is where God works in the unseen.

I have had seasons where I begged for movement. I wanted signs, doors, and clarity. But all I got was silence. And in that silence, I learned to listen differently. I discovered that God does not just speak through miracles; He whispers through stillness.

"But those who wait on the Lord shall renew their strength..." Isaiah 40:31

Waiting builds strength. It deepens trust. It strips away the need for control and teaches you to rest in divine timing. The wilderness is not punishment; it is preparation.

Faith Lesson

God is not slow; He is strategic. What feels like a delay is often development. He is not just preparing the blessing; He is preparing you to carry it.

When I finished my Doctorate, I was uncertain about my next steps. I was out of full-time permanent work from January 2014 to December 2016. Should I take on a director role? A full-time faculty position? Or combine a director's role with part-time faculty work? I was trying to find my way.

Spiritually, I felt called to move, so I began applying for positions outside Connecticut. In 2018, an accounting faculty position opened in the Bronx, New York, but I still had ties to Connecticut. For a while, I commuted between the states, teaching in New York in the morning and returning to Connecticut to fulfill other responsibilities. These were not permanent roles, but I needed income, work experience, and clarity on my next step.

By 2019, I was offered a high-level executive position in a southern state. This started my rise and success in leadership roles aligned with my profession, accounting. This season taught me that delay is not denial, waiting does not mean "never."

Waiting was crucial. It gave me time to heal, prepare, and seek God through prayer and fasting. It shaped my character, strengthened my faith, and clarified my purpose. By the time the right opportunity arrived, I was ready to step fully into that role.

Reflection Prompt

What are you waiting for right now? Write down how this season is shaping your character, faith, and perspective. What might God be teaching you in the quiet?

Closing Prayer

Lord, help me to trust You in the waiting. Teach me to see Your hand even when I do not see movement. Strengthen me, shape me, and prepare me for what is next. Amen.

CHAPTER EIGHT:

WHO AM I WITHOUT THE LABELS?

We live in a world that loves to define us by what we do: student, parent, entrepreneur, artist, leader. But what happens when the job ends, the relationship shifts, or the season changes? Who are you then?

I had a moment where everything I thought defined me was gone. The title, the platform, the applause, all faded. And in that silence, I heard God whisper:

"You are mine. That is enough."

"Before I formed you in the womb, I knew you..." Jeremiah 1:5

Your identity is not earned; it is inherited. You are chosen, loved, and called, not because of what you do, but because of who He is.

Faith Lesson

When you know who you are in Christ, you stop chasing validation from the world. You walk in confidence, not comparison. You lead from overflow, not emptiness.

Growing into who you are meant to be is a shift. It is a pivot. It is a turn. I carry titles, doctorate, adjunct professor, accountant, writer, author, teacher, and more, but what do they truly mean? They are tools, not definitions. The real purpose lies in what I do with them: serving, teaching, and producing lasting fruit.

"Ye have not chosen me, but I have chosen you, and ordained you, that ye should go and bring fruit, and that your fruit

should remain that whatsoever ye shall ask of the Father in my name, He may give it to you." — John 15:16

I am enough. I was called for a specific purpose: to go forth and bring forth fruit. Even if I stripped away all titles, I would still teach, serve, and provide wisdom, both spiritually and naturally, because I am God's child.

"So, God created mankind in His own image..." — Genesis 1:27
"If anyone is in Christ, the new creation has come..." — 2 Corinthians 5:17
"You are a chosen people... God's special possession..." — 1 Peter 2:9

These verses remind us: we are crafted with intention, made new, and chosen not by merit but by grace.

Prayer of Identity

God,
Strip away the noise, the names, the roles.
Let me stand before You as I am—
Not what I do, not what I have earned, not what others see.
I am Yours.
Formed by Your breath,
Held in Your gaze,
Loved without condition.

In the quiet, I remember:
I am not forgotten.
I am not mistaken.
I am not alone.
I am known.
I am chosen.
I am enough.

Let me live from this place—
Not chasing worth but resting in it.
Not performing but abiding.
Not hiding but shining.

Amen.

Reflection Prompt

What labels have you been carrying that no longer serve you? Write them down, then cross them out. Beneath them, write who God says you are, beloved, redeemed, and enough.

____

____

____

____

____

Closing Prayer

Lord, remind me who I am when the world tries to tell me otherwise. Strip away every false label and replace it with Your truth. Help me to walk boldly in the identity You have given me. Amen.

CHAPTER NINE:
WHEN THE FIRE FADES

You can love God deeply and still feel exhausted. You can serve faithfully and still feel empty. Burnout does not mean you are broken; it means you have been burning too long without rest.

I have had seasons where I showed up, smiled, and led, but inside, I was numb. I did not want to quit, but I did not know how to keep going. In that fragile place, God did not demand more from me. He whispered:

"Come to Me. I will give you rest." – Matthew 11:28

God does not need your performance. He wants your presence. He is not asking you to push harder; He is inviting you to breathe deeper.

Faith Lesson

Rest is holy. Sabbath is sacred. You do not recharge by doing more; you heal by being still. Burnout is not failure; it is a signal to return to the Source.

When the plug is pulled on your life and circumstances, it is time to rest. I recall being both an administrator and an adjunct professor at the same time. The environment was toxic, and I remember a new co-worker asking why it was so negative. I told her the truth: it wasn't natural, it was spiritual. It was culture shock, and God's timing was perfect to close all doors in that environment for me.

This happened during the dissertation phase of my doctorate. I decided to finish my dissertation while working part-time and consulting. The negativity and pressure had drained me, but it also created space to slow down. I took time to rest, visit family, care for myself, and focus on my studies. I reviewed my finances and realized I could support myself without returning to full-time work.

If I could go back, I would tell myself:

"Self, it is okay to rest. To restore. To relieve stress. To care for you. Opportunities will come, and God will bring you higher."

And He did. God elevated me to higher leadership positions, proving that rest is not retreat; it is preparation.

"I know thy works: behold, I have set before thee an open door, and no man can shut it." — Revelation 3:8

"But those who wait on the Lord shall renew their strength; they shall mount up with wings like eagles; they shall run and not be weary; they shall walk and not faint." — Isaiah 40:31

Reflection Prompt

Where have you been running empty? Write down the areas of your life that feel heavy. Then ask yourself: What would rest look like here? What boundaries need to be rebuilt?

___

___

___

___

___

Closing Prayer

Lord, I am tired, not just physically, but spiritually. Meet me in this weariness. Restore my joy, renew my strength, and remind me that I do not have to carry it all. Amen.

CHAPTER TEN:

THE FREEDOM OF LETTING GO

There is a weight that does not show up on scales: resentment. It sits quietly in your spirit, whispering reminders of betrayal, hurt, and injustice. I carried it for years. I thought holding on gave me power. But it only gave me pain.

Then one day, God whispered: *"You're not protecting yourself; you're imprisoning yourself."*

Forgiveness was never about them; it was about me. It was about my healing, my freedom, my ability to move forward.

"Forgive, and you will be forgiven." — Luke 6:37

Forgiveness does not mean what happened was okay. It means choosing peace over poison. It is not weakness; it is warfare. It is how you reclaim your joy.

Faith Lesson

Unforgiveness is a spiritual clog. It blocks blessings, clarity, and peace. Forgiving is not for the other person; it is for you. I had to forgive myself to step into the next level of my life; to lighten the load I had been carrying for years.

Some lessons came through hurt: to strengthen me, to help me see hidden enemies, to protect myself, and to release those who could not journey with me into the next realm.

In this season, I am forgiving and letting go:

- Friends who did not support me.
- Exes who were absent when I needed them.

- Family members who were unsupportive or critical.
- Neighbors who tried to sway me from my path.
- Employers who demanded more than the job required.
- Anyone who offended me in any way.
- And most importantly, I am forgiving myself for trusting others too freely, for not setting boundaries, for carrying too much weight.

I am releasing it all. I am thanking God for forgiving me, too.

"Brethren, I do not count myself to have apprehended; but one thing I do, forgetting those things which are behind and reaching forward to those things which are ahead, I press toward the goal for the prize of the upward call of God in Christ Jesus." — Philippians 3:13-14

"Old things have passed away; behold, all things have become new." 2 Corinthians 5:17

"Many are the afflictions of the righteous, but the Lord delivers him out of them all." — Psalms 34:19

"Let us lay aside every weight, and the sin which so easily ensnares us, and let us run with endurance the race that is set before us." — Hebrews 12:1

Reflection Prompt

Who do you need to forgive, even if they never apologize? Write their name. Then write: *"I release you."* You do not have to feel it yet; start the process.

___

___

___

___

___

Closing Prayer

Lord, I have been holding on to pain. Help me release it. Teach me to forgive like You do, fully, freely, and faithfully. Heal my heart, restore my peace, and help me walk in freedom. Amen.

CHAPTER ELEVEN:
OBEDIENCE OVER UNDERSTANDING

God does not always explain Himself. Sometimes he says, *"Go."* And you are left wondering, *"Go where? Why now? What if I fail?"* But obedience is not about having all the answers; it is about trusting the One who does.

I have had moments when the next step felt irrational: leaving the job, starting something new, forgiving that person. Every time, I wrestled with logic. But obedience is not logical; it is spiritual. It is surrender in motion.

"Trust in the Lord with all your heart and lean not on your own understanding." — Proverbs 3:5

Obedience unlocks blessings that understanding cannot. It is the key to divine alignment, even when the path feels uncertain.

Faith Lesson

Delayed obedience is disobedience. When God speaks, He is not asking for perfection; He is asking for movement. Your *"yes"* is the seed of a breakthrough. At this stage in my journey, I am pivoting, taking it step by step, stepping into the next level of educating and writing.

"Behold, to obey is better than sacrifice." — 1 Samuel 15:22

Obedience is better than sacrifice (1 Samuel 15:22). I remember after completing my doctorate, I was working in NYC and Connecticut simultaneously. A high-level executive position opened in the South. I got the job, passed the background check, agreed to the salary, and had a start date. Yet as the date approached, there was no word from the employer or onboarding person.

By this time, I had seen enough chaos, backstabbing, and blocking spirits. My spirit told me I was supposed to be in the South, but fear made me hesitate. I told myself: I cannot stay traveling between two states working part-time; I need benefits. I had two part-time jobs lined up for the New Year.

The Spirit nudged me: fly to the nearest city where the job is and call them the day before you start. I knew something didn't feel right, but I moved in faith. I encouraged myself to go, knowing the only thing I could lose was a plane ticket.

I spent New Year's Eve in a neighboring southern city, celebrating, I then called the onboarding person the next day. Their hesitation confirmed my doubts. When I arrived, the CEO said, *"I'm so glad you came. I talked about you during the holidays with my family, and they said you weren't coming from up North. I'm so glad you are here."*

My faith and obedience had been rewarded. I received the higher salary I requested, not the lower one I was told. From there, I went on to greater exploits. I had a feeling that the onboarding person "*forgot to call me and send the paperwork,*" so I just showed up. I wasn't going to take no for an answer, so, instead of calling anyone, I showed up. God showed out!!!

Sometimes you cannot stay where you are. It requires trusting God in the process. It takes courage, faith, discernment, and obedience to move in the right direction.

"Obedience is spiritual. It is believing without seeing. It is an expectation without knowing."

"For we walk by faith, not by sight." — 2 Corinthians 5:7

"If you are willing and obedient, you shall eat the good of the land." — Isaiah 1:19

Reflection Prompt

What has God asked you to do that you have been hesitating on? Write it down; Then write: *"I choose obedience."* Even if it is scary. Even if it is slow.

Closing Prayer

Lord, I do not always understand Your ways, but I trust Your heart. Provide the courage to obey, even when it is uncomfortable. Align my steps with Your will. Amen.

CHAPTER TWELVE:

BEAUTY FROM BROKENNESS

Pain has a way of making you question everything, your faith, your worth, your future. I have walked through seasons where the hurt felt louder than hope. But in the middle of that ache, God whispered, *"I'm still writing."*

Pain does not mean God has left. It means He is working in deeper places. The cracks in your heart are not signs of failure; they are places where light can get in.

"And we know that in all things God works for the good of those who love Him..." – Romans 8:28.

God does not waste wounds. He repurposes them. What broke you might be the very thing that builds someone else. Your story becomes someone else's survival guide.

Faith Lesson

Pain is a platform. It teaches compassion, deepens wisdom, and births purpose. Do not rush past it, redeem it. This is exactly where I am today, letting go of the old and moving into the new. I am trusting God in the purposes He has for me, telling the stories of how He brought me out and carried me through. I now know that my journey from the "projects to purpose" was always part of His plan.

Many doors I walked through, except GE, were with strangers. The people I expected to support me often did not. Some are not called to align with you. Nothing is wrong with them; they are not a part of your assignment. But God taught me an important truth: *What He has for me is mine. My name is on it.* Every opportunity and every open door with my name on it is mine. God gives, God prepares, and God sends the helpers when needed. One of my prayers now is simple but powerful: *"Lord, send me my helpers."*

Many opportunities came from people pointing me in the right direction, others I met along my journey, and some I met at an event, which prepared me for opportunistic doors. I am grateful to all who have given me a hand up along the way. I appreciate the favor of God over my life.

As I move forward, I can see the shift in my approach. Where I once worked out of desperation to provide for my family, I now choose opportunities that align with my purpose. I am walking into the promise God has prepared for me.

"To give unto them beauty for ashes..." — Isaiah 61:3

God will give you beauty for ashes. He will take your breakdown and use it for His glory. As Psalms 3:3 reminds us, *"But You, LORD, are a shield around me, my glory, the One who lifts my head high."*

Reflection Prompt

What painful season have you walked through that shaped you? Write down what it taught you, and how it might help someone else. Remember: your scars are sacred.

____

____

____

____

____

Closing Prayer

Lord, I do not always understand the pain, but I trust you to use it. Heal what is broken, redeem what is lost, and create beauty from my ashes. Amen.

CONCLUSION:
THE JOURNEY WAS NEVER JUST ABOUT YOU

You have walked through comparisons, closed doors, seasons of waiting, identity shifts, burnout, forgiveness, obedience, and pain. And through it all, one truth has echoed: God never left.

This was not just a collection of chapters; it was a soul excavation. A reminder that your story is sacred, your scars are sermons, and your steps are ordered. You did not just survive, you grew. You did not just learn, you transformed.

"Being confident of this, that He who began a good work in you will carry it on to completion..." — Philippians 1:6

Final Faith Lesson

Your life is a living testimony. Every detour, delay, and disappointment was a setup for a deeper purpose. You are walking in grace, covered in mercy, and called to impact. You are not behind. You are not forgotten. You are not disqualified. You are becoming.

I wrote this book to share my story, to show how God brought me from the projects into doors I never could have dreamed of. There was no blueprint for me to follow. My neighborhood was not sending most of its youth to colleges or universities. But I used my love of books and magazines like *Essence*, *Jet*, and *Black Enterprise*, to imagine a different life. They showed me that success was possible.

As a teenager, I made mistakes that made me question my dreams. Yet, I surpassed even my own expectations, achieving the heart's desire of attending college. It was a journey filled with twists, turns, and difficulties, but God was always guiding me. Even in the blessings, I carried past traumas, feelings of abandonment, guilt, and self-punishment. But I am forgetting those things which are behind me and pressing forward. I am excited to see what this next chapter looks like for me. God always satisfies with good things.

Moving Into Purpose:

- Shifting within.
- Reaping blessings from the battle.
- Identifying your power.
- Removing comparisons.
- Dancing at the closed door.
- Waiting for confirmation from God.
- Removing labels.
- Taking rest before the next.
- Letting go of the past.
- Being obedient to God,
- Accepting beauty for ashes,
- Finally, moving on...next!

Final Reflection Prompt

Write a letter to your future self. Remind them of what you have overcome, what you have learned, and what you now believe. Seal it with this truth: *"I am still becoming."*

____

____

____

____

____

Final Prayer

Lord, thank You for every chapter. Thank You for staying close in the chaos and whispering truth in the silence. I trust you with my story. I surrender the pen. Write something beautiful. Amen.

Psalms 23

The Lord is my shepherd; I shall not want.
He makes me lie down in green pastures; He leads me beside the still waters.
He restores my soul; He leads me in the paths of righteousness for His name's sake.
Yea, though I walk through the valley of the shadow of death, I will fear no evil.

For You are with me; Your rod and Your staff, they comfort me.
You prepare a table before me in the presence of my enemies.

You anoint my head with oil; My cup runs over.
Surely goodness and mercy shall follow me all the days of my life.

And I will dwell in the house of the Lord forever.

YOUR NEXT STEPS

Thank you for reading, *What God Has for Me is Mine: It Has My Name on It!*

I hope this book has encouraged you, reminded you of your purpose, and inspired you to walk boldly into the blessings God has prepared just for you.

Remember: What God has for you is yours; it has your name on it!

To help you further, look for the accompanying journal: *What God Has for Me Is Mine*. It is designed to guide your reflections, prayers, and declarations as you apply the lessons from this book.

I'd love to hear from you! Share your thoughts, breakthroughs, or questions—your story might inspire someone else.

Email: thecoachingcreator@gmail.com

Website Coming Soon: www.thecoachingcreator.com.

Keep moving in faith, trusting God's timing, and stepping fully into the life He has called you to. The best is still ahead!

With gratitude and encouragement,

Dr. Tonia Ann Walker

www.ingramcontent.com/pod-product-compliance
Lightning Source LLC
LaVergne TN
LVHW041256150826
845673LV00008B/2613

* 9 7 9 8 9 9 4 8 0 4 2 0 9 *